A VIRTUOUS WOMAN'S PRAYER

IS

JESUS

FILL MY CUP

YOU SHALL NEVER THIRST AGAIN

My hope and prayer is that when you finish reading this book, you will no longer feel empty and have that thirst in your mind, spirit and soul. God is going to quench your thirst. He is going to fill your cup with all His benefits because you are His beloved daughter. God wants to talk to you while filling your cup. So, listen to Him!

A PERSONAL WEEKLY FOCUS, SCRIPTURE, DECLARATION, PRAYER AND ENCOURAGING MESSAGE

YOLANDA MARSHALL-NICKERSON

CONTENTS

INTRODUCTION..

WEEK 1 ABUNDANCE
....9

WEEK 2 ANOINTING
....11

WEEK 3 ADVANCEMENT
....13

WEEK 4 AUTHORITY
....17

WEEK 5 BALANCE
....19

WEEK 6 BLESSINGS
....23

WEEK 7 BREAKTHROUGH
....27

WEEK 8 CARE
....31

WEEK 9 CHARACTER
....33

WEEK 10 CONFIDENCE
....37

WEEK 11 CHANGE
.... 41

WEEK 12 CHEER
....45

WEEK 13 COMMUNICATION
....49

WEEK 14 COURAGE
....53

WEEK 15 DIRECTION
....55

WEEK 16 DISCERNMENT
....59

WEEK 17 DESTINY
....63

WEEK 18 FAITH
....67

WEEK 19 FAVOR

....71

WEEK 20 GOODNESS
....73

WEEK 21 GRACE
....77

WEEK 22 HAPPINESS
....79

WEEK 23 HARVEST
....81

WEEK 24 INCREASE
....83

WEEK 25 INTEGRITY
....85

WEEK 26 JOY
....87

WEEK 27 KNOWLEDGE
....89

WEEK 28 LOVE
....93

WEEK 29 MERCY
....95

WEEK 30 PATIENCE
....97

WEEK 31 POWER
....99

WEEK 32 PURPOSE
....101

WEEK 33 PEACE
....103

WEEK 34 PRAISE
...................................105

WEEK 35 PERSERVERANCE
...............................107

WEEK 36 PRAYER
....111

WEEK 37 RIGHTEOUSNESS
....113

WEEK 38 REST
....115

WEEK 39 RESTORATION
....117

WEEK 40 SECURITY

....119

WEEK 41 SELF-CONTROL

....121

WEEK 42 STRENGTH

....125

WEEK 43 TRUST

....127

WEEK 44 TENACITY

....129

WEEK 45 THANKSGIVING

....133

WEEK 46 UNDERSTANDING

....135

WEEK 47 VISION

....139

WEEK 48 VICTORY

....141

WEEK 49 WISDOM

....143

WEEK 50 WORSHIP

....145

WEEK 51 WORTH

....147

WEEK 52 ZEAL

....149

INTRODUCTION

Some of us cannot seem to start our day off without having a cup of coffee, tea or hot chocolate. Seemingly these things give us a brain booster and they warm some of us who are cold natured. We crave these and other things because we have latched on to the fact that these things really do work for us. We wouldn't dare think that any of these things would cause us harm. We believe they will always work; that's why we continue to fill our cups with them every morning.

While we fill our natural cups with these and other things, we must understand that our spiritual cups need to be filled daily. Some of our spiritual cups are empty, and some of us have allowed our spiritual cups to be filled with things that have no real meaning—the things of the world that make us feel depressed, oppressed, angry, bitter, and the list goes on.

I want you to know that there is One who can and will fill your spiritual cup with everlasting things; One who will cause you to never thirst again; One who rewards those who seek and believe in Him —His name is Jesus. He will help you shift your focus off the problems that you will encounter on your life's journey and direct your attention toward a powerful solution that will work for you every day—PRAYER—this is your direct communication with Him. What a privilege and honor it is to know and have a relationship with the One who can hear and answer your and everyone else's prayer request at the very same time! He never sleeps nor slumbers.

You can access Him all day, every single day of your life. He will never ignore you or turn His back on you. This book provides a prayer focus for every week of the year, and you can experience the spiritual essence of each of these things, which should be every human being's desire from day to day. Say this before you go any further: I shall never thirst again.

WEEK ONE

ABUNDANCE

Focus: This week I encourage you to meditate on abundance.

Scripture: "Now unto him that is able to do exceeding abundantly above all that we ask or think..." (Ephesians 3:20)

Declaration: I will live in abundance, and it shall spill over into the lives of those who are connected to me.

Prayer: God, I pray that You allow me to experience abundance according to Your riches and glory. I understand that everything belongs to You, and I know that You will not withhold anything from me because I am Your child. Amen.

Message: It is your time to experience abundance. It is the will of God that you have more than enough because He is "more than enough." He is majesty. He is awesome. He is miraculous. He is extraordinary, and He does supernatural things. He is all that any of us can ask for at any given time. His abundance will always transcend every area of lack that you may experience in your life. You can go ahead and tell lack good-bye and welcome abundance—this is your entitlement through Jesus Christ! Stay Encouraged! Stay Motivated! Stay Close to God! Have a blessed week!

YOUR PERSONAL NOTE TO GOD

_____

_____

_____

_____

_____

_____

_____

_____

_____

_____

_____

_____

_____

_____

_____

_____

_____

_____

_____

_____

_____

_____

WEEK TWO

ANOINTING

Focus: This week I encourage you to meditate on anointing.

Scripture: "...The yoke shall be destroyed because of the anointing." (Isaiah 10:27)

Declaration: I will forever cherish the anointing that God has poured upon my life.

Prayer: God, I pray that You allow me to experience Your anointing on every level. I believe in the power of Your anointing and trust that it will be used to destroy every attack that will come against me. Amen.

Message: The anointing is in essence a great power that God will bestow upon your life. There is nothing (circumstance, problem, concern...) that can match that kind of power. As you meditate on the scripture mentioned above, you will find that the anointing is so strong to where it can destroy anything. You may encounter negative things that may try to work against you this week, but just know that it will not defeat you because the anointing will defeat it. God is getting ready to increase the level of anointing that is on your life. Stay Encouraged! Stay Motivated! Stay Close to God! Have a blessed week!

YOUR PERSONAL NOTE TO GOD

WEEK THREE

ADVANCEMENT

Focus: This week I encourage you to meditate on advancement.

Scripture: "Then the king promoted Daniel and gave him many great gifts; and he made him ruler over the whole province of Babylon..." (Daniel 2:48)

Declaration: I am going from level to level. Advancement is a part of God's plan for my life.

Prayer: God, I pray that You open more doors for me. I understand that when You open a door in my life, no man or woman can close it. I realize that when You are ready to advance me, no one can stop it. I am positioning myself to receive my advance ticket to a world of opportunities for Your glory. Amen.

Message: God wants you to live a good life. He wants you to receive all that He has for you. God wants to take you from one position to another; from one level to another; from low to high. He does not want you to be stagnated. I want you to think about where you are now in your life and where you want to go, what you want to obtain, and how you can position yourself for elevation. Always remember to put God first in all matters of

A VIRTUOUS WOMAN'S PRAYER IS JESUS FILL MY CUP

your life. He wants to advance, promote you, and you can count on Him to do it real soon. Stay Encouraged! Stay Motivated! Stay Close to God! Have a blessed week!

YOUR PERSONAL NOTE TO GOD

_____

_____

_____

_____

_____

_____

_____

_____

_____

_____

_____

_____

_____

_____

_____

_____

_____

_____

_____

_____

_____

_____

_____

_____

_____

WEEK FOUR

AUTHORITY

Focus: This week I encourage you to meditate on authority.

Scripture: "And they were astonished at His teaching, for His Word was with authority." (Luke 4:32)

Declaration: I will use the authority God has given me to speak into the atmosphere and command everything in my life to line up according to His will.

Prayer: God, I pray that You give me Holy boldness to speak against the things that are not of You; the things that I shouldn't think about submitting to; the things that are not right in Your sight. Amen.

Message: Sometimes in life you will face things that are so enticing, yet they are not good for you. You will need to stand boldly on God's Word and take authority over any ungodly thought and/or thing that will try to captivate your attention and bind you. Jesus was in authority and He spoke His Word with it, and you are His daughter, so you too can do the same. This week, I encourage you to put God's Word on that situation and command it to line up…Stay Encouraged! Stay Motivated! Stay Close to God! Have a blessed week!

YOUR PERSONAL NOTE TO GOD

_____

_____

_____

_____

_____

_____

_____

_____

_____

_____

_____

_____

_____

_____

_____

_____

_____

_____

_____

_____

_____

_____

_____

_____

WEEK FIVE

BALANCE

Focus: This week I encourage you to meditate on balance.

Scripture: "Rest in the Lord and wait patiently for Him." (Psalm 37:7)

Declaration: I will have balance in my life. I will not allow anything or anyone to cause me to be on the go often as I need to, and I will not be consumed with matters that don't require my attention and efforts.

Prayer: God, I pray that You help me to have balance in my life. I realize that I am human and need to get appropriate rest to maintain a healthy lifestyle. Amen.

Message: I want you to think about what you can eliminate doing this week. You should prioritize the most important to the least important. If it is too much for you to get done this week, then you need to rearrange your schedule. You are not a robot. You are a human being, and every human has to have time to rest. Think about this: God created the Heaven and Earth, and He took a day to rest; that means He didn't do anything. This should be enough for you to realize that you are not superwoman and that you need to have some balance in your

A VIRTUOUS WOMAN'S PRAYER IS JESUS FILL MY CUP

life. Always remember that it is perfectly okay to say no to people sometimes. And you can say no without letting others make you feel guilty about not being able to commit to doing something they may ask you to do.

Having balance in your life should not ever be contingent upon whether someone else has balance in their life. You have to learn to do things that are better and healthier for you. Stay Encouraged! Stay Motivated! Stay Close to God! Have a blessed week!

YOUR PERSONAL NOTE TO GOD

_____

_____

_____

_____

_____

_____

_____

_____

_____

_____

_____

_____

_____

_____

_____

_____

_____

_____

_____

_____

_____

_____

WEEK SIX

BLESSINGS

Focus: This week I encourage you to meditate on blessings.

Scripture: "Blessed shall you be in the city, and blessed shall you be in the country." (Deuteronomy 28:3)

Declaration: I am about to receive all the blessings that my name is attached to.

Prayer: God, I pray that You continue pouring Your blessings upon my life. I realize that You are at the helm of every blessing that I have and will ever receive. I honor You for all that You have done for me and thank You in advance for what You will continue doing for me. Amen.

Message: At some point in life you may have heard someone say that "God is in the blessing business." If you haven't heard it before, let me be the first to tell you that He is the leader of blessings; nobody else can bless like Him. As you go to God in prayer about blessings this week, think about what He has already blessed you with and have faith that He will continue to pour His blessing upon you. One thing that I know for sure is that God does not have a shortage of blessings. The beauty about our Heavenly Father is that He can bless you unlimited; that means the blessings will never stop. Go ahead and expect

A VIRTUOUS WOMAN'S PRAYER IS JESUS FILL MY CUP

to be "blessed by the Best" again and again! You deserve to receive that blessing (healing, promotion, job, house, car, etc.) that you have been petitioning God for. Stay Encouraged! Stay Motivated! Stay Close to God! Have a blessed week!

YOUR PERSONAL NOTE TO GOD

_____

_____

_____

_____

_____

_____

_____

_____

_____

_____

_____

_____

_____

_____

_____

_____

_____

_____

_____

_____

_____

_____

WEEK SEVEN

BREAKTHROUGH

Focus: This week I encourage you to meditate on breakthrough.

Scripture: "The Lord will grant you plenty of goods...And the Lord will open to you His good treasure, the heavens, to give the rain to your land in this season and to bless all the work of your hand." (Deuteronomy 28:11-12)

Declaration: I am about to experience a right now breakthrough.

Prayer: God, I pray that You allow me to experience a breakthrough this week. I have encountered many obstacles, but I do believe in Your power. I know that Your power is greater than any obstacle. I know that my breakthrough is near. Amen.

Message: It is time for your breakthrough moment. You have been through enough hell. You have been fighting long enough. You have been crying long enough. You have been in lack long enough. You have been stagnated long enough. You have been in the valley long enough. You have been sick long enough. You have been broke long enough. You have been confused long enough. You have been stressed long enough. You have been emotionally weak long enough. You have been lied on and lied to long enough. You have been in bondage long enough. I

A VIRTUOUS WOMAN'S PRAYER IS JESUS FILL MY CUP

want you to know that God does not get any pleasure out of your being in a place of sorrow.

It is time for you to experience the power of God like never before while you are here on earth. He is going to deliver you from bondage and propel you to your place of breakthrough. You can go ahead and receive it in your spirit. Stay Encouraged! Stay Motivated! Stay Close to God! Have a blessed week!

YOUR PERSONAL NOTE TO GOD

_____

_____

_____

_____

_____

_____

_____

_____

_____

_____

_____

_____

_____

_____

_____

_____

_____

_____

_____

_____

_____

_____

_____

_____

WEEK EIGHT

CARE

Focus: This week I encourage you to meditate on care.

Scripture: "Let nothing be done through selfish ambition or conceit, but in lowliness of mind let each esteem others better than himself. Let each of you look out not only for his own interest, but also for the interests of others." (Philippians 2:3-4)

Declaration: I will be sensitive to others and show that I do care and not only be concerned with what's going on in my life.

Prayer: God, I pray that You allow people to see You in me, through my caring heart. Amen.

Message: It is rather easy to think about only yourself at times. You can often forget about others, what they are going through, and a need that they might have. I encourage you to think about someone else's needs this week. Show that you care about others by simply praying for someone, giving someone a hug, buying someone food, giving someone clothing or shoes, etc. It shows just how big your heart is and that your thoughts are genuine and pure when you can do for others without someone nudging you to do so. More importantly, it shows that you care and would do just as Jesus Christ would do. Stay Encouraged! Stay Motivated! Stay Close to God! Have a blessed week!

YOUR PERSONAL NOTE TO GOD

_____

_____

_____

_____

_____

_____

_____

_____

_____

_____

_____

_____

_____

_____

_____

_____

_____

_____

_____

_____

_____

_____

WEEK NINE

CHARACTER

Focus: This week I encourage you to meditate on character.

Scripture: "Let this mind be in you which was also in Christ Jesus..." (Philippians 2:5)

Declaration: I will strive for perfection and be mindful of what I say and do, in and out of the sight of others.

Prayer: God, I pray that You build my character. I want to become more like You every day. Lord, help me to become more cognizant of what I say and what I do. I realize that people are watching me, and I desire for them to see You in me at all times. I want my actions to reflect who You really are in my life. Amen.

Message: What are people saying about your character? Do you really believe that others are watching seemingly everything you do? Do you feel like sometimes you are under a microscope being examined for any wrongdoing? If you feel this way, then it is true that others are always watching, and they either have a positive or negative perception of you. It seems as though people are waiting for you to make a wrong turn in life, make a bad decision, as if you are a perfect being. None of us have arrived at the level of perfection, and I don't

A VIRTUOUS WOMAN'S PRAYER IS JESUS FILL MY CUP

think that we will ever experience perfection while here on earth. However, I do believe that we can lead a godly life (publicly and privately) where people can see the essence of Jesus in us; more importantly, we want God to be pleased with us.

He's the One that sees every move we make because "He sits high and looks low." I encourage you to petition God for help in the area of character building. In order to become a better person and strive for perfection, your character may need to be sharpened a little; therefore, let the One who made you and knows all about you start the process. Once He starts the character building process, others will see the difference in you, and they will know that you've been touched by God. Stay Encouraged! Stay Motivated! Stay Close to God! Have a blessed week!

YOUR PERSONAL NOTE TO GOD

_____

_____

_____

_____

_____

_____

_____

_____

_____

_____

_____

_____

_____

_____

_____

_____

_____

_____

_____

_____

_____

_____

WEEK TEN

CONFIDENCE

Focus: This week I encourage you to meditate on confidence.

Scripture: "I will praise You, for I am fearfully and wonderfully made. "(Psalm 139:14)

Declaration: I am confident in me, and I will hold my head up high, knowing that God created me in His own image; knowing that I can do all things through Him, according to His Word. I am a beautiful Gem and God loves me.

Prayer: God, I pray that You help me to see myself as You see me and be confident in the "skin that I am in," as Your fearfully and wonderfully made daughter. Amen.

Message: If you are struggling with having confidence, I encourage you to simply start looking in the mirror and say to yourself: No longer shall I belittle myself or lack confidence in my abilities, talents, or gifts. When you are not confident in yourself, you not only limit your abilities…you also limit God. You should never limit God because He is the One who created you, and He gave you the power to get wealth, the knowledge to get the job done, and the gifts and talents to become successful in life. As a child of God, everything that you aspire to do should be done with confidence, and it will prosper if you

A VIRTUOUS WOMAN'S PRAYER IS JESUS FILL MY CUP

trust the One who gave you the mindset to do it. Every person you encounter should be able to look at you and know that you are a confident woman and not a woman of fear and low self-esteem. Stay Encouraged! Stay Motivated! Stay Close to God! Have a blessed week!

YOUR PERSONAL NOTE TO GOD

_____
_____
_____
_____
_____
_____
_____
_____
_____
_____
_____
_____
_____
_____
_____
_____
_____
_____
_____
_____
_____
_____
_____
_____
_____
_____

WEEK ELEVEN

CHANGE

Focus: This week I encourage you to meditate on change.

Scripture: "Because the carnal mind is enmity against God..." (Romans 8:7)

Declaration: I am going to make a conscience effort to change every day.

Prayer: God, I pray that You help me to change daily. My mind, my soul, my spirit, and my heart's desire are to be like You, Lord. I know that with You I can change, and I am ready to change. Amen.

Message: When you desire change in your life, then you are simply tired of your old ways. You have come to know that doing the same thing produces the same results; doing un-productive, ungodly things can lead you down a path to nowhere. You no longer want to operate with a carnal mind. You have tried it the devil's way and found that it hasn't helped you on your journey; it has only handicapped you and impeded your movement. Now you are ready to do things God's way because you believe that you can move forward and prosper all the days of your life. Desiring change suggests that you want to be different, make a difference and go in a different

A VIRTUOUS WOMAN'S PRAYER IS JESUS FILL MY CUP

direction—the direction in which God leads you. You want to experience everything that He has for you. You no longer want to be hindered by anyone or anything.

You want to grow and please God in all that you do. I want to let you know that greater lies ahead of you because you desire more. You want to contribute more. You deserve more. And you shall receive more. Watch how "God perfect that which concerns you," because of your willingness to change! Stay Encouraged! Stay Motivated! Stay Close to God! Have a blessed week!

A VIRTUOUS WOMAN'S PRAYER IS JESUS FILL MY CUP

YOUR PERSONAL NOTE TO GOD

_____
_____
_____
_____
_____
_____
_____
_____
_____
_____
_____
_____
_____
_____
_____
_____
_____
_____
_____
_____
_____
_____
_____
_____

WEEK TWELVE

CHEER

Focus: This week I encourage you to meditate on cheer.

Scripture: "...Jesus spoke to them, saying, "Be of good cheer!"(Matthew 14:27)

Declaration: I will not be moved by the things that are going on around me. I will be of good cheer for the rest of my life.

Prayer: God, I pray that You continue to allow me to have a cheerful spirit, even when trouble is all around me. I know that as long as You are with me, I will be safe and secure. Amen.

Message: You may be dealing with something in your life right now that is seemingly trying to get the best of you. The devil may have told you that you are in trouble and there is no way of escape. I want you to know that the "devil is the father of lies," and he just wants you to be moved by your situation and circumstances. He wants you to live in fear and have doubt. You have to tune him out as often as he comes in your life to cause chaos. Have faith in knowing that there is no trouble you will ever face on earth that Jesus cannot get you out of. God specializes in delivering His children from those things that bind them. There is always a way of escape when you have Jesus walking by your side. Therefore, don't let whatever the

A VIRTUOUS WOMAN'S PRAYER IS JESUS FILL MY CUP

issue is keep your spirit down. Rejoice in the Lord! God has not failed you yet. Just as Jesus told His disciples, He is telling you the same thing, "Be of good cheer!" Stay Encouraged! Stay Motivated! Stay Close to God! Have a blessed week!

YOUR PERSONAL NOTE TO GOD

_____

_____

_____

_____

_____

_____

_____

_____

_____

_____

_____

_____

_____

_____

_____

_____

_____

_____

_____

_____

_____

_____

_____

_____

WEEK THIRTEEN

COMMUNICATION

Focus: This week I encourage you to meditate on communication.

Scripture: "Let no corrupt word proceed out of your mouth, but what is good for necessary edification, that it may impart grace to the hearers." (Ephesians 4:29)

Declaration: I will strive to communicate in a positive manner daily, casting down every thought that exalt itself against God—negative thoughts that produce negative words.

Prayer: God, I pray that You help me to communicate in a positive manner, putting a bridle on my tongue when I am at the brink of saying something that I shouldn't say. Your Word says that life and death is in the power of my tongue; therefore, I only desire to speak life from this day forward. Amen.

Message: Do you ever feel like saying something that you shouldn't say? Aren't you glad that you have a God that can and will control your tongue when those negative words spring forth and are at the brink of flowing through your lips? I encourage you to continue feeding your spirit with positivity and make sure you surround yourself with people who are positive and uplifting. Once you build off positivity, you will

A VIRTUOUS WOMAN'S PRAYER IS JESUS FILL MY CUP

then speak only those words that will uplift people and not tear them down. Yes, even when people despitefully use you, hurt you or abuse you, it is a must that you remain positive and keep your character in check.

Remember, God wants you to respond in a positive manner; that is why you should partner with Him and pray continuously that He controls your tongue because you can easily say something that you may regret, and you can never take back words (good or bad) after they flow through your lips. Be cognizant of the way you communicate this week if you should happen to face a situation that may tempt you to react in a negative manner. Stay Encouraged! Stay Motivated! Stay Close to God! Have a blessed week!

YOUR PERSONAL NOTE TO GOD

_____

_____

_____

_____

_____

_____

_____

_____

_____

_____

_____

_____

_____

_____

_____

_____

_____

_____

_____

_____

_____

WEEK FOURTEEN

COURAGE

Focus: This week I encourage you to meditate on courage.

Scripture: "...Be strong and of good courage...." (Deuteronomy 31:7)

Declaration: I believe that God will give me the courage to carry out what He has put in my spirit to do.

Prayer: God, I pray that You give me the courage to "be all that I can be" for Your glory. Amen.

Message: There is absolutely no task that God has instructed you to do, that He will not equip you to handle, even as it relates to your career, raising your children or something else. He will give you the strength and courage to execute. God will not have you clueless or wondering how you're going to get the job done or how the provision will be made. He is the One who will go before you and prepare the way. He will be with you. "He will never leave you nor forsake you. Do not fear nor be dismayed." Trust God and have courage, woman! Stay Encouraged! Stay Motivated! Stay Close to God! Have a blessed week!

YOUR PERSONAL NOTE TO GOD

_____

_____

_____

_____

_____

_____

_____

_____

_____

_____

_____

_____

_____

_____

_____

_____

_____

_____

_____

_____

_____

_____

_____

_____

WEEK FIFTEEN

DIRECTION

Focus: This week I encourage you to meditate on direction.

Scripture: "The steps of a good man are ordered by the Lord, and He delights in his way." (Psalm 37:23)

Declaration: I will follow God's direction and not my own because I know where He guides me; it will be where He wants me to be at that appointed time.

Prayer: God, I pray that You lead me on my life's journey. You know where You desire for me to be, how long You want me to be there, and how You want me to get from one destination to the next. I pray that I never pick my own direction to take because it may lead to a path of destruction. Order my steps, Lord! I trust Your leading. Amen.

Message: Have you ever prayed for God's directions, but you ended up taking a wrong turn in life that led to a dead end because you thought that your way was the better way? I am certain if you did you felt some kind of way. You may have had an uneasy, lonely feeling. You may have even felt like you had made one of the biggest mistakes in your life after learning that you were in the wrong place at the wrong time. I want you to know that just because you made a wrong turn (maybe even

A VIRTUOUS WOMAN'S PRAYER IS JESUS FILL MY CUP

recently) in life that led you to a dead end, does not mean that God would leave you there alone. He will meet you at the dead end, embrace you, and let you know that you're at the wrong place. He will remind you that you are His daughter and put you back on the right path that leads to destiny.

From this day forward, I encourage you to let God start leading you. He is the only One who can go before you and "make the crooked places straight." Don't travel in a direction on your own because it may be to your hurt, and God doesn't want that for you. Listen to Him and be patient with Him and trust His direction for your life. He will safely get you from point A to B, from one destination to the next, without any stumbling blocks. Stay Encouraged! Stay Motivated! Stay Close to God! Have a blessed week!

YOUR PERSONAL NOTE TO GOD

_____
_____
_____
_____
_____
_____
_____
_____
_____
_____
_____
_____
_____
_____
_____
_____
_____
_____
_____
_____
_____
_____
_____
_____

WEEK SIXTEEN

DISCERNMENT

Focus: This week I encourage you to meditate on discernment.

Scripture: "A wise man's heart discerns..." (Ecclesiastes 8:5)

Declaration: I will use discernment for every matter in my life.

Prayer: God, I pray that You give me the spirit of discernment. I understand that there are a lot of things going on around me. The world is in such an uproar and wickedness is seemingly at its highest, Lord. I want to be able to discern the time and be vigilant as I know the devil is working, roaming the earth seeking whom he may devour. Amen.

Message: We are living in a world where there is seemingly everything going on around us. There are people who don't give a care in the world, from those in your family to those in the workplace to those in the church, etc. Many people are doing all kinds of evil things, and the devil is at the helm of those things. The devil wants to deceive anyone that he can while roaming the earth. You have to gird yourself with the truth, the Word of God. Get close to Him, stay in His presence and seek Him for discernment so that you won't be deceived! With the spirit of discernment, you are able to tap into the spiritual realm. You may have experienced a level of

A VIRTUOUS WOMAN'S PRAYER IS JESUS FILL MY CUP

discernment already; perhaps, you may have felt the urge (or had that "gut" feeling) not to go to a certain place or take a certain route to work or something else—that was that still small voice of Jesus speaking to you, allowing you to go around trouble, if you will.

Let your prayer include God sharpening your level of discernment this week. He will always hear the effectual, fervent prayers of the righteous. Stay Encouraged! Stay Motivated! Stay Close to God! Have a blessed week!

YOUR PERSONAL NOTE TO GOD

_____

_____

_____

_____

_____

_____

_____

_____

_____

_____

_____

_____

_____

_____

_____

_____

_____

_____

_____

_____

_____

_____

WEEK SEVENTEEN

DESTINY

Focus: This week I encourage you to meditate on destiny.

Scripture: "So when Samuel saw Saul, the Lord said to him...this one shall reign over my people." (1 Samuel 9:17)

Declaration: I believe that I can walk in my destiny with God on my side because He is at the helm of my destiny.

Prayer: God, I pray that You help me focus on my destiny. I know that You have great things for me to do, and You have purposed me for destiny. I know that You already defeated the devil on Calvary, so he doesn't control my destiny. You are the only One who holds the key to my destiny. Amen.

Message: Your life was already mapped out before you were ever thought about being conceived. You can rest assure that your destiny is a sure thing. When people call you unworthy, unqualified, untalented, unimportant, God calls you a blessed child of His who is destined for awesome, wonderful, great things. You are purposed to carry out a particular assignment for God, and He has already equipped you for it, and it is part of your destiny. I encourage you to seek God about where you need to go from this point in your life and ask Him to help you

A VIRTUOUS WOMAN'S PRAYER IS JESUS FILL MY CUP

get to your destiny. When He speaks to you concerning your destiny, make sure you heed His voice. He'll never steer you wrong. Stay Encouraged! Stay Motivated! Stay Close to God! Have a blessed week!

YOUR PERSONAL NOTE TO GOD

_____

_____

_____

_____

_____

_____

_____

_____

_____

_____

_____

_____

_____

_____

_____

_____

_____

_____

_____

_____

_____

_____

_____

_____

WEEK EIGHTEEN

FAITH

Focus: This week I encourage you to meditate on faith.

Scripture: "Now faith is the substance of things hoped for, the evidence of things not seen." (Hebrews 11:1)

Declaration: I will strive to operate in faith in every situation.

Prayer: God, I pray that You build my faith. I want to walk by faith and not by sight. I realize that You are moved by my faith and not by my complaints nor by fear. Amen.

Message: Sometimes when your back is up against the wall, when all hell breaks loose, when trouble appears to be on every side of you, when your bills are past due and you have no money to pay them, when you are sick in your body, when your relationship is in an uproar, when you're facing problems on your job...that is when your faith is tested and much needed, yet it is weaken because of all that is going on in your life. It seems like it's very hard for you to have faith because of fear of what may happen while you're dealing with so much at one time. I encourage you to hold steadfast and don't let your problems get the best of you. Don't let the devil make you lose faith and give up on God. The devil thrives off fear, but you got to tell him to get behind you. I want you to know that God works at His best

A VIRTUOUS WOMAN'S PRAYER IS JESUS FILL MY CUP

and can perform miracles when you are dealing with so many unfavorable things at the same time; when you feel like He is nowhere near you or have a care about your situation. He sees and He cares.

He just wants you have that "mustard seed faith." The Bible shares with us the story of the woman who had the issue of blood for 12, long, dreary years. When the woman touched the hem of Jesus' garment, she was made whole. Her healing manifested through her faith. Having faith is very key and you must activate it this week, woman! (Read Luke, Chapter 8). Stay Encouraged! Stay Motivated! Stay Close to God! Have a blessed week!

YOUR PERSONAL NOTE TO GOD

_____
_____
_____
_____
_____
_____
_____
_____
_____
_____
_____
_____
_____
_____
_____
_____
_____
_____
_____
_____
_____
_____

WEEK NINETEEN

FAVOR

Focus: This week I encourage you to meditate on favor.

Scripture: "...His favor is for life." (Psalm 30:5)

Declaration: I will experience God's favor all the days of my life. He will also grant me favor with everyone that I come in contact with on my journey.

Prayer: God, I pray that You grant me uncommon favor. I know that it is a privilege and honor to be favored by You. I want to experience Your favor daily. Amen.

Message: There is no devil in hell or on earth that can block God's favor on your life. Because of God's favor on your life, you will experience supernatural things that some others may not ever experience. Since you are favored by God, you can get ready to be moved to the front of the line. No longer shall you be in the back of the line; no longer shall you be last. Position yourself to start moving this week to the front... "Eyes have not seen, nor ear heard...the things that He has prepared for those who love Him." I encourage you to continue carrying out your purpose, keep walking upright, and keep being obedient to His Word. Stay Encouraged! Stay Motivated! Stay Close to God! Have a blessed week!

YOUR PERSONAL NOTE TO GOD

_____

_____

_____

_____

_____

_____

_____

_____

_____

_____

_____

_____

_____

_____

_____

_____

_____

_____

_____

_____

_____

_____

WEEK TWENTY

GOODNESS

Focus: This week I encourage you to meditate on goodness.

Scripture: "...the goodness of God endures continually." (Psalm 52:1)

Declaration: I believe that You will allow me to continue experiencing Your goodness, Lord.

Prayer: God, I am so grateful for Your goodness. I realize that I haven't been deserving of Your goodness many times in life. But, I am glad that You see the depths of my heart and have looked past every mistake that I have ever made. You're awesome, Lord. Amen.

Message: If you examine your past experiences, you may find that you haven't always done everything right. You fell short of God's glory many, many times—but, the God we serve picked you up! He kept you in the midst of adversity; while you were in your mess. His goodness transcends every mistake that you have (and will make) made, and I am certain that you are glad about that. I encourage you to stay on course and strive to lead a positive, godly life. Don't succumb to the foolish, wicked things of the world. Don't let anyone get you off track and don't allow yourself to fall prey to the devil's tricks. God wants

A VIRTUOUS WOMAN'S PRAYER IS JESUS FILL MY CUP

to do so many wonderful things in your life, and He wants to continue showing you His goodness. You deserve everything that He has in store for you. Stay Encouraged! Stay Motivated! Stay Close to God! Have a blessed week!

YOUR PERSONAL NOTE TO GOD

_____

_____

_____

_____

_____

_____

_____

_____

_____

_____

_____

_____

_____

_____

_____

_____

_____

_____

_____

_____

_____

_____

WEEK TWENTY-ONE

GRACE

Focus: This week I encourage you to meditate on grace.

Scripture: "And God is able to make all grace abound toward you..." (2 Corinthians 9:8)

Declaration: I believe that God will continue to make His grace abound toward me.

Prayer: God, I pray that You continue pouring Your grace on me. I pray that You have mercy on me, too. Lord, take me around any danger and keep a shield of protection around me forevermore. Amen.

Message: The grace of God is with you every day, and the Bible tells us, "His grace is sufficient." When you pray to God throughout this week, ask Him to not only show His grace toward you, but ask Him to show His grace toward your unsaved family members, friends, and coworkers. God's grace exceeds every mistake and sin that you have and will commit in your life. I don't want you to think that it is okay to sin though; you must steer away from living any kind of lifestyle and knowingly sinning and doing wrong. I encourage you to make a personal commitment to do what's right. Stay Encouraged! Stay Motivated! Stay Close to God! Have a blessed week!

YOUR PERSONAL NOTE TO GOD

_____

_____

_____

_____

_____

_____

_____

_____

_____

_____

_____

_____

_____

_____

_____

_____

_____

_____

_____

_____

_____

_____

WEEK TWENTY-TWO

HAPPINESS

Focus: This week I encourage you to meditate on happiness.

Scripture: "...Happy are the people whose God is the Lord."(Psalm 144:15)

Declaration: I will maintain a level of happiness every day. I will not succumb to anything that will cause me to be unhappy.

Prayer: God, I pray that You bless me to experience happiness every day of my life. I believe that I can experience happiness with You as my Lord. Steer me away from the things and people that will try to make me unhappy, Lord. Amen.

Message: Have you had more sad moments than happy moments? Perhaps, you may be experiencing sadness right now. You must remember that God wants you to rejoice and be happy in life. Sure, there are times when you may feel a little down, but you cannot stay there and allow yourself to become depressed. If the devil had his way, he will always make you feel depressed, sad, angry, or miserable. You have to learn to be happy when "all odds are against you." Take back your happiness and make up your mind this week that you are going to stay happy! Stay Encouraged! Stay Motivated! Stay Close to God! Have a blessed week!

YOUR PERSONAL NOTE TO GOD

_____

_____

_____

_____

_____

_____

_____

_____

_____

_____

_____

_____

_____

_____

_____

_____

_____

_____

_____

_____

_____

_____

_____

WEEK TWENTY-THREE

HARVEST

Focus: This week I encourage you to meditate on harvest.

Scripture: "While the earth remains, seedtime and harvest..." (Genesis 8:22)

Declaration: I am next in line for my harvest to manifest.

Prayer: God, I thank You in advance for my harvest. I pray that You continue to bless me with seed to sow into Your work. Amen.

Message: You can have confidence in knowing that God is the One who makes it possible for you to receive a harvest, an overflow, where your cup will run over with His blessings. I believe that you are in a season where you will experience the harvest. "God will always give seed to the sower." I decree that your finances are about to turn around. Your body is in the process of being healed. Your spiritual gifts and talents are about to make room for you. More doors are about to open for you. Your purpose is about to be revealed. It's not just a matter of time; it's your time. The harvest is yours. Claim it and receive it in your spirit! Stay Encouraged! Stay Motivated! Stay Close to God! Have a blessed week!

YOUR PERSONAL NOTE TO GOD

_____
_____
_____
_____
_____
_____
_____
_____
_____
_____
_____
_____
_____
_____
_____
_____
_____
_____
_____
_____
_____
_____
_____
_____

WEEK TWENTY-FOUR

INCREASE

Focus: This week I encourage you to meditate on increase.

Scripture: "May the Lord give you increase more and more..." (Psalm 115:14)

Declaration: I will experience God's increase like never before, and I am ready for all that He has in store for me.

Prayer: God, I pray for increase and I thank You in advance for an increase in every area of my life. Amen.

Message: As you walk in your harvest season, go ahead and embrace an increase in every area of your life—mentally, emotionally, financially, and spiritually. God wants to do this just for you. It is God's will for your life. It is your right as a child of God to have all that He has for you. I decree, "No more lack," in your life. This week tell God about your needs and trust Him to provide every one of them. God has more than enough for every need that you have for your family, your ministry, your business, etc. Stay Encouraged! Stay Motivated! Stay Close to God! Have a blessed week!

YOUR PERSONAL NOTE TO GOD

_____

_____

_____

_____

_____

_____

_____

_____

_____

_____

_____

_____

_____

_____

_____

_____

_____

_____

_____

_____

_____

_____

_____

WEEK TWENTY-FIVE

INTEGRITY

Focus: This week I encourage you to meditate on integrity.

Scripture: "Let integrity and uprightness preserve me, for I wait for you..." (Psalm 25:21)

Declaration: I will strive each day to walk in integrity.

Prayer: God, I pray that You help me to walk in integrity daily and be a woman of my word. Amen.

Message: It is so important that you have integrity in your home, on your job, in your community—when people are watching and when they are not watching you. Even more, God always has His eyes on you, and He knows your thoughts and sees your actions. Sometimes God will allow certain things to happen in your life to see how you're going to respond and whether you're going to do the right thing in the midst of that situation. I encourage you to do what's right when others don't want to, when no one is watching you, and even when it hurts. You must also ensure that you are keeping commitments that you make and honoring your word that you give to someone, too. If you lack integrity, ask God to help you every day to be a person of integrity. He will do it for you. Stay Encouraged! Stay Motivated! Stay Close to God! Have a blessed week!

YOUR PERSONAL NOTE TO GOD

_____

_____

_____

_____

_____

_____

_____

_____

_____

_____

_____

_____

_____

_____

_____

_____

_____

_____

_____

_____

_____

_____

WEEK TWENTY-SIX

JOY

Focus: This week I encourage you to meditate on joy.

Scripture: "...My joy may remain in you, and your joy may be full..." (John 15:11)

Declaration: I will no longer allow anything to steal my joy.

Prayer: God, I thank You that my joy is found in You. I pray that I experience joy every day. Amen.

Message: You can consider it being the devil's assignment to throw all kinds of things at you within a day to steal your joy. The devil is your enemy and he doesn't want you to be full of joy. I encourage you to lean on God every day and make sure you put Him first when you wake up every morning. Before you leave your home, you need to say, "This is the day the Lord has made. I will rejoice and be glad in it." When you say this you are echoing the Word of God into the atmosphere and confirming the kind of day you're going to have. Therefore, no matter what the devil tries to do, it will not work. It will not shake, break, move or steal your joy. I decree that you will have a joyful week. It shall be so. Stay Encouraged! Stay Motivated! Stay Close to God! Have a blessed week!

YOUR PERSONAL NOTE TO GOD

_____
_____
_____
_____
_____
_____
_____
_____
_____
_____
_____
_____
_____
_____
_____
_____
_____
_____
_____
_____
_____
_____
_____
_____
_____
_____

WEEK TWENTY-SEVEN

KNOWLEDGE

Focus: This week I encourage you to meditate on knowledge.

Scripture: "Wise people store up knowledge..." (Proverbs 10:14)

Declaration: I will strive every day to gain more knowledge on my journey in life.

Prayer: God, I pray that You increase my knowledge. Give me the eagerness to learn more and feed my spirit by reading Your Word, other books and materials that will be helpful to me and my growth in life. Amen.

Message: You may have heard that "Knowledge is power." That is definitely a known fact. I encourage you to get to that place where you have a desire to gain more knowledge so that you cannot be easily swayed or deceived by the devil through people and/or miss opportunities that require a certain level of knowledge. There are times when you may have taken what people have told you at face value; not knowing if it was true or untrue. You may not have gone back to try to discover the truth because it didn't have a direct impact on you. If you are now working you may realize that your employer has more confidence in you when they know you have understanding and

A VIRTUOUS WOMAN'S PRAYER IS JESUS FILL MY CUP

knowledge of your role. Having knowledge is not only important, but it is very beneficial to you.

The Bible tells us that it is basically a wise thing to have knowledge. Gain more knowledge and grow even more! It's an awesome thing to do. Stay Encouraged! Stay Motivated! Stay Close to God! Have a blessed week!

YOUR PERSONAL NOTE TO GOD

_____

_____

_____

_____

_____

_____

_____

_____

_____

_____

_____

_____

_____

_____

_____

_____

_____

_____

_____

_____

_____

_____

_____

_____

WEEK TWENTY-EIGHT

LOVE

Focus: This week I encourage you to meditate on love.

Scripture: "This My commandment, that you love one another as I have loved you." (John 15:12)

Declaration: I will have agape love toward everyone as God has commanded me to do.

Prayer: God, I pray that You teach me how to love myself and all mankind just as You love me and everyone else. Amen.

Message: Have you ever been hurt to the point to where you felt like you didn't have the heart to love that person or people unconditionally anymore? I want you to know that there are times in life when some people will say and do things to intentionally hurt you, but some will do and say things to unintentionally hurt you. Either way, you cannot let it cause you to become bitter because bitterness can lead to hate. You don't want this to happen. The devil is the face behind hatred. You have to still love people who mistreat you on any level because this is a commandment given by God. If you feel that you lack love, God will show you how to love people the way He desires for you to. Stay Encouraged! Stay Motivated! Stay Close to God! Have a blessed week!

YOUR PERSONAL NOTE TO GOD

_____

_____

_____

_____

_____

_____

_____

_____

_____

_____

_____

_____

_____

_____

_____

_____

_____

_____

_____

_____

_____

_____

_____

_____

WEEK TWENTY-NINE

MERCY

Focus: This week I encourage you to meditate on mercy.

Scripture: "...For His mercy endures forever." (1 Chronicles 16:34)

Declaration: I will stand on God's mercy forevermore.

Prayer: God, I thank You for having mercy on me. Amen.

Message: God is merciful to all of us. He has brought us through some of the most difficult times in our lives. Pause right there and give Him praise! He is so worthy of our praise. I am certain that if you reflect upon your past experiences and all the negative things that you have gone through, you know that it was nothing else but God's "grace and mercy that brought you through..." It is such a blessing to know that you can count of God's mercy; knowing that it will never run out. What a wonderful, spiritual benefit to have as a child of God! I encourage you to keep grace and mercy as your best friends because they will be there when everyone else turns their back on you. Stay Encouraged! Stay Motivated! Stay Close to God! Have a blessed week!

YOUR PERSONAL NOTE TO GOD

_____

_____

_____

_____

_____

_____

_____

_____

_____

_____

_____

_____

_____

_____

_____

_____

_____

_____

_____

_____

_____

_____

_____

_____

_____

WEEK THIRTY

PATIENCE

Focus: This week I encourage you to meditate on patience.

Scripture: "Rest in the Lord, and wait patiently for Him..." (Psalm 37:7)

Declaration: I will be patient and wait on the Lord.

Prayer: God, I pray that You help me to be patient so that I will not move too fast and make a mistake that may have an adverse effect on my life. Amen.

Message: God wants you to practice patience concerning every area of your life. He doesn't want you to be so impatient to the point to where your emotions lead to your making critical decisions that may cause harm to you. He doesn't want you to get ahead of Him. He wants you to just follow Him and trust His judgment. You must realize that His timing is the right time for things to happen in your life; whether it be getting married, starting a business, or anything else that we often rush into doing. I know you've been praying and believing God for that particular thing, and you can barely wait for it to happen. I encourage you to relax and be patient and know that "He's turning it around for you." Stay Encouraged! Stay Motivated! Stay Close to God! Have a blessed week!

YOUR PERSONAL NOTE TO GOD

_____

_____

_____

_____

_____

_____

_____

_____

_____

_____

_____

_____

_____

_____

_____

_____

_____

_____

_____

_____

_____

_____

_____

_____

WEEK THIRTY-ONE

POWER

Focus: This week I encourage you to meditate on power.

Scripture: "...He who gives strength and power to His people." (Psalm 68:35)

Declaration: I will walk in the authority of God and use the power He has given me to trample the devil anytime he tries to attack me.

Prayer: God, I pray that You pour Your power upon me. Amen.

Message: "Greater is He that is in you; than he (the devil) that is in the world." When you latch on to the fact that God is within you and that "there is power in the name of Jesus," then you will not fear what the devil may even try to do to you. The devil is very powerless, and he cannot do anything with God. He was defeated on Calvary before your existence. I encourage you to use the power that God has given you to trample and combat the devil's attacks, even in the battle that you may now find yourself facing—you got the power to fight. Know that you are not in that battle alone; God is right there fighting with you. Stay Encouraged! Stay Motivated! Stay Close to God! Have a blessed week!

YOUR PERSONAL NOTE TO GOD

_____

_____

_____

_____

_____

_____

_____

_____

_____

_____

_____

_____

_____

_____

_____

_____

_____

_____

_____

_____

_____

_____

WEEK THIRTY-TWO

PURPOSE

Focus: This week I encourage you to meditate on purpose.

Scripture: "...But for this purpose I came to this hour. Father, glorify Your name." (John 12:27)

Declaration: I will carry out my purpose and glorify my Heavenly Father.

Prayer: God, I pray that You reveal to me Your purpose for my life, so that I can fulfill it. Amen.

Message: God knew all about you before you were born, and you were created with a purpose. You may already know what your purpose is; you may be executing the task God specifically told you to do. If you have not already connected with your purpose, I encourage you to seek God wholeheartedly about it. He will reveal it to you. Whether you know it or not, He has bestowed certain spiritual gifts upon you, and those gifts are to be used to carry out your purpose, glorifying God in all that you do. As you carry out your assignment, make sure you never ever seek glory for yourself. Your purpose is all about God, and He wants all the glory. Stay Encouraged! Stay Motivated! Stay Close to God! Have a blessed week!

YOUR PERSONAL NOTE TO GOD

_____

_____

_____

_____

_____

_____

_____

_____

_____

_____

_____

_____

_____

_____

_____

_____

_____

_____

_____

_____

_____

_____

_____

_____

_____

WEEK THIRTY-THREE

PEACE

Focus: This week I encourage you to meditate on peace.

Scripture: "Peace I leave with you, My peace I give to you..." (John 14:27)

Declaration: I will experience the peace of God daily.

Prayer: God, I pray that Your peace surpass every circumstance and situation in my life. Amen.

Message: There will be times when you may face some things that will try to snatch your peace, but you have to hold on to your peace during those turbulent times. God gave you His peace; therefore, He doesn't want you to be troubled, enduring the stresses of life's ups and downs. In order to have a peace of mind, you have to continuously feed your spirit with His Word, pray without ceasing and declaring that you will have peace no matter what comes your way. I encourage you to start thinking peace when you wake every morning and even when lie down every night. I decree that the peace of God be released and saturate the discomforting place that you may now find yourself in. Stay Encouraged! Stay Motivated! Stay Close to God! Have a blessed week!

YOUR PERSONAL NOTE TO GOD

WEEK THIRTY-FOUR

PRAISE

Focus: This week I encourage you to meditate on praise.

Scripture: "Let everything that has breath praise the Lord. (Psalm 150:6)

Declaration: I will praise the Lord every day.

Prayer: God, I pray that You lift any burdens that may try to prevent me from giving You praise. Amen.

Message: If you have breath in your body, there shouldn't ever be a reason you shouldn't praise God. He is always deserving of every ounce of praise that lies within your soul. The devil hates it when you praise God, but He loves it when you praise him; that is why he launches his attacks daily. The devil wants you to give attention to those attacks and keep saying, "the devil did this; the devil did that to me." Don't give the devil anymore praise. Give praise to God. Your praise is one of the spiritual keys that will unlock the door to your blessings, miracles, supernatural, extraordinary favor. There are some things that you have been standing in the need of that is going happen for you this week, and your praise to God is going to make it possible. Praise ye the Lord, woman! Stay Encouraged! Stay Motivated! Stay Close to God! Have a blessed week!

YOUR PERSONAL NOTE TO GOD

_____
_____
_____
_____
_____
_____
_____
_____
_____
_____
_____
_____
_____
_____
_____
_____
_____
_____
_____
_____
_____
_____
_____
_____
_____
_____

WEEK THIRTY-FIVE

PERSERVERANCE

Focus: This week I encourage you to meditate perseverance.

Scripture: "...Knowing that tribulation produces perseverance, and perseverance, character; and character, hope." (Romans 5:3-4)

Declaration: I am going to persevere until the end for I know that tough times definitely won't last until the end.

Prayer: God, I pray that You give me the strength that I need to endure any obstacle that may be designed to get me off track. I know that there is nothing too hard for You, Lord. Amen.

Message: Some people said that you were not going to make it when you were faced with certain trials and tribulations, but you managed to make it, with God's help. When some people "wrote you off" and said that you should have been dead by now, God said something totally different about you. He said, "You shall live and not die and declare His works," and that's why you are still here. There is something in your spirit that is pushing you forward, and there is purpose deep within your soul. I encourage you to keep moving because victory is ahead of you. I want you to know that God is always working behind the scene on your behalf, and He is about to reveal

A VIRTUOUS WOMAN'S PRAYER IS JESUS FILL MY CUP

Himself in a special way and bless you just because you are His child. Your perseverance is surely not in vain. Keep praying! Keep pushing! Keep believing! Don't give up now, woman. "The best is yet to come." Stay Encouraged! Stay Motivated! Stay Close to God! Have a blessed week!

YOUR PERSONAL NOTE TO GOD

_____

_____

_____

_____

_____

_____

_____

_____

_____

_____

_____

_____

_____

_____

_____

_____

_____

_____

_____

_____

_____

_____

WEEK THIRTY-SIX

PRAYER

Focus: This week I encourage you to meditate on prayer.

Scripture: "...The effective, fervent prayers of a righteous man availeth much." (James 5:16)

Declaration: I will make my daily request known to my Heavenly Father through prayer.

Prayer: God, I ask that You increase my desire to pray every day of my life. Amen.

Message: There may have been times when you only depended on someone else to pray for you, but it is so very important that you have a prayer life. It is also great to have a prayer partner as the Bible tells us that when two people come together asking for anything, it shall be done by Him (Read Matthew 18:19). I encourage you to set aside some quiet time daily and go into prayer. God wants to hear from you; therefore, you have to make it personal with Him every day. You don't want to just only pray when you are facing difficult times. You want to pray at all times. Consider it a privilege and an honor to have the One who cannot only hear your prayers, but answer your prayers, at any time of day or night! Stay Encouraged! Stay Motivated! Stay Close to God! Have a blessed week!

YOUR PERSONAL NOTE TO GOD

WEEK THIRTY-SEVEN

RIGHTEOUSNESS

Focus: This week I encourage you to meditate on righteousness.

Scripture: "...Hear me when I call, O God of my righteousness." (Psalm 4:1)

Declaration: I will walk upright before the Lord daily.

Prayer: God, I pray that You help me to live an upright life. I realize that I cannot do this on my own. I need You to sustain me when sin shows its' face. Amen!

Message: I want you to know that you are honoring God when you live righteously, "laying aside every weight and sin that so easily ensnares you...." You have to make sure you partner with God to help you stay on the right, narrow path in life. You can never do it by yourself because your flesh is always going to war with your spirit. You may fall short of His glory sometimes, but when your heart's desire is to do the right thing, God will not allow you to be comfortable in sin. When the devil tempts you to sin, you have to resist him every time. The Bible tells us not to give the devil any place in our lives. If you are in a web of sin now, I want you to know that God can deliver you and put you back on the right track. Stay Encouraged! Stay Motivated! Stay Close to God! Have a blessed week!

YOUR PERSONAL NOTE TO GOD

_____

_____

_____

_____

_____

_____

_____

_____

_____

_____

_____

_____

_____

_____

_____

_____

_____

_____

_____

_____

_____

_____

_____

WEEK THIRTY-EIGHT

REST

Focus: This week I encourage you to meditate on rest.

Scripture: "Come to Me, all you who labor and are heavy laden, and I will give you rest."(Matthew 11:28)

Declaration: I will rest in the Lord and give Him all of my cares.

Prayer: God, I pray that You give me rest in my flesh and in my spirit while You work this situation out for me. Amen.

Message: I believe that you can rest in the Lord right here on earth. What I mean by this is that you can release all of your concerns and cares of the world to God, and He can give you rest in your spirit and in your flesh while you are going through your trials and tribulations. You may be currently dealing with something on your job, in your home, in your church, etc., but one things' for sure, God is all, knows all, and has all the solutions to your problems—everything that you are dealing with. I want you to know that God is going to work it out for you, not just this time, but every time you face something that is designed to disturb your mind, spirit and soul, and steal your peace and joy. Stay Encouraged! Stay Motivated! Stay Close to God! Have a blessed week!

A VIRTUOUS WOMAN'S PRAYER IS JESUS FILL MY CUP

YOUR PERSONAL NOTE TO GOD

_____
_____
_____
_____
_____
_____
_____
_____
_____
_____
_____
_____
_____
_____
_____
_____
_____
_____
_____
_____
_____
_____
_____

WEEK THIRTY-NINE

RESTORATION

Focus: This week I encourage you to meditate on restoration.

Scripture: "So I will restore to you the years that the swarming locust has eaten..." (Joel 2:25)

Declaration: I will receive everything the devil stole from me.

Prayer: God, I pray for restoration. I believe that You will give me "double for my trouble," triple for my shame, an overflow of blessings. Amen.

Message: You may have lost some things on your journey, but you can be assured that your name is on God's to be restored list. The devil slowly took from you and troubled you mentally, emotionally, physically, financially and spiritually over an extended period of time, but God is going to quickly and suddenly restore to you the years....you are going to have more than enough joy, peace, happiness, strength, finances, etc. God is going to make sure you get back everything the devil stole from you. You can go ahead and put a smile on your face. I decree that you shall start seeing and receiving those things this week. Stay Encouraged! Stay Motivated! Stay Close to God! Have a blessed week!

YOUR PERSONAL NOTE TO GOD

WEEK FORTY

SECURITY

Focus: This week I encourage you to meditate on security.

Scripture: "...When the enemy comes in like a flood, the spirit of the Lord will lift up a standard against him." (Isaiah 59:19)

Declaration: I have security as long as I have Jesus.

Prayer: God, I pray that You build a fence around me and keep me away from all harm and danger. Amen.

Message: God is on alert 24 hours a day, and He will come to your rescue when you are in danger. Stress not about your enemies or what they can do to you. The adversary's (devil) mission is to destroy you, and he will try to use anything or anyone to complete his task. I encourage you to have faith in what Jesus can and will do for you, and that is fight every one of your battles. You don't have to depend on anyone else to provide security for you. God is your safety net. He is your protector. He is your shield. He is your army. He will keep you. He is the watchman of your soul. As stated before, "God doesn't slumber nor sleep. He will preserve you from all evil. He shall preserve your soul...your going out and coming in..." Stay Encouraged! Stay Motivated! Stay Close to God! Have a blessed week!

YOUR PERSONAL NOTE TO GOD

_____

_____

_____

_____

_____

_____

_____

_____

_____

_____

_____

_____

_____

_____

_____

_____

_____

_____

_____

_____

_____

_____

_____

WEEK FORTY-ONE

SELF-CONTROL

Focus: This week I encourage you to meditate on self-control.

Scripture: "But the fruit of the Spirit is love, joy, peace, longsuffering, kindness, goodness, faithfulness, self-control......" (Galatians 5:22)

Declaration: I will have self-control over every matter in my life.

Prayer: God, I pray that You help me to have self-control, preventing me from operating in my flesh, but in the spirit. Amen.

Message: You can easily find yourself losing control if you are not in the spirit when faced with certain situations. We are all subject to act in a negative manner if we are operating in the flesh. If you are currently dealing with negative minded people on your job who offends you often, I encourage you to ask God to help you maintain control in that situation. If you are dealing with a situation at home with your spouse or children, and you're at the brink of exploding, I encourage you to ask God to help you maintain control in that situation. If you are dealing with a situation at church where there is disagreement or confusion, and you feel like you want to tell someone what's

A VIRTUOUS WOMAN'S PRAYER IS JESUS FILL MY CUP

really on your mind, I encourage you to ask God to help you maintain control in that situation.

Whatever the situation is that you may be facing, I encourage you not to lose control, but have self-control. You will always be in control when you release your concerns to the One, Jesus Christ, who is in control of your life. Stay Encouraged! Stay Motivated! Stay Close to God! Have a blessed week!

YOUR PERSONAL NOTE TO GOD

_____
_____
_____
_____
_____
_____
_____
_____
_____
_____
_____
_____
_____
_____
_____
_____
_____
_____
_____
_____
_____
_____
_____
_____
_____

WEEK FORTY-TWO

STRENGTH

Focus: This week I encourage you to meditate on strength.

Scripture: "The Lord will give strength to his people..." (Psalm 29:11)

Declaration: I will use the strength of God to get through my trials and tribulations.

Prayer: God, I pray that You allow me to lean on Your strength always. Amen.

Message: Some things in life may cause some of the strongest of people to feel extremely low in spirit. How much more can one feel that is not so strong, especially spiritually, when life throws them a curve ball! If you are in a place of depression, I want you to know that God is going to give you that much needed strength to press on. See, you're more than a conqueror. Most importantly, you are a child of God, and He has already given you the victory over every matter in your life. That heavy load that you are carrying is about to be lifted. Just keep the faith and depend on Him. The Word of God tells us that "His yoke is easy and His burden is light." (Read Matthew 11:30). Stay Encouraged! Stay Motivated! Stay Close to God! Have a blessed week!

YOUR PERSONAL NOTE TO GOD

_____
_____
_____
_____
_____
_____
_____
_____
_____
_____
_____
_____
_____
_____
_____
_____
_____
_____
_____
_____
_____
_____
_____

WEEK FORTY-THREE

TRUST

Focus: This week I encourage you to meditate on trust.

Scripture: "Trust in the Lord with all your heart..." (Proverbs 3:5)

Declaration: I will trust the Lord forevermore.

Prayer: God, I pray that You help me to trust You with all my heart and place the things that I am faced with in Your hands. Amen.

Message: You should always trust God because He is the only One who will never fail you. At some point in life you may have found yourself in a certain situation, and you needed people to come to your rescue. It seems as though everywhere you looked and turned, no one was there, not even those who you thought you could trust to be in your corner, praying for you. Don't ever find it strange when people fail you; it will happen sometimes in life. This is when you have to know without a shadow of doubt that God is and should be the only One who you need to trust 100 percent. He wants you to trust Him with that matter that you have been trying to figure out. Release it to Him and let Him take care of it. Stay Encouraged! Stay Motivated! Stay Close to God! Have a blessed week!

YOUR PERSONAL NOTE TO GOD

_____

_____

_____

_____

_____

_____

_____

_____

_____

_____

_____

_____

_____

_____

_____

_____

_____

_____

_____

_____

_____

_____

_____

_____

WEEK FORTY-FOUR

TENACITY

Focus: This week I encourage you to meditate on tenacity.

Scripture: "I can do all things through Christ who strengthens me." (Philippians 4:13)

Declaration: I will not give up this time. I will complete the task that is set before me.

Prayer: God, I pray that You give me the tenacity to do the things that You have instructed me to do, and given me the power to do, according to Your will. Amen.

Message: Oftentimes things will come against you and try to hinder you from doing something that God has instructed you to do, and given you the power to do. You may find yourself struggling with getting the job done. I want you to know that no matter how hard it may seems or how weary you may become, I encourage you not to give up. God didn't give you the spirit of fear nor the will to quit. You have the power to tread the devil when he comes to your mind and tell you that you ought to just quit because God is not going to guide you through, and even when people make you feel like you're not capable or smart enough to complete the task. The devil is a liar. God is with you and He will give you the tenacity to push

A VIRTUOUS WOMAN'S PRAYER IS JESUS FILL MY CUP

forward and complete the task that you have started. Stay Encouraged! Stay Motivated! Stay Close to God! Have a blessed week!

YOUR PERSONAL NOTE TO GOD

_____

_____

_____

_____

_____

_____

_____

_____

_____

_____

_____

_____

_____

_____

_____

_____

_____

_____

_____

_____

_____

_____

_____

_____

_____

_____

WEEK FORTY-FIVE

THANKSGIVING

Focus: This week I encourage you to meditate on thanksgiving.

Scripture: "Let us come before his presence with thanksgiving and make a joyful noise until him…" (Psalm 95:2)

Declaration: I will always show and tell the Lord how thankful I am for who He is and for what He has done for me.

Prayer: God, I pray that You keep my heart full of gratitude. Amen.

Message: You will have some good days and bad days on earth, but through it all, you can still tell God how much you appreciate and thank Him. Every morning He blesses you to open your eyes, you should say, "Thank You, Lord." God is the One who makes it possible for you to have food on your table, clothes on your back, shoes on your feet, a sound mind, health and strength, and all the other natural things you need to survive. He is the One who will come to your rescue when you are in trouble; the One who will heal your body when you're sick; the One who will make your enemies act right; the One who will show you grace and mercy when you get out of His will. He is all that each of us need. Stay Encouraged! Stay Motivated! Stay Close to God! Have a blessed week!

YOUR PERSONAL NOTE TO GOD

_____

_____

_____

_____

_____

_____

_____

_____

_____

_____

_____

_____

_____

_____

_____

_____

_____

_____

_____

_____

_____

_____

_____

WEEK FORTY-SIX

UNDERSTANDING

Focus: This week I encourage you to meditate on understanding.

Scripture: "Trust in the Lord with all your heart, and lean not to your own understanding." (Psalm 119:73)

Declaration: I will use the understanding God has given me every day.

Prayer: God, I pray that You increase my level of understanding and not allow me to lean to my own understanding. Amen.

Message: It is very important that you have a spiritual understanding, but it is also important that you have a general understanding of certain things, as well as people. However, it is never okay to lean to your own understanding. Oftentimes if you lean to your own understanding, you are bound to make a bad decision that could possibly lead to a negative outcome. If you don't have a spiritual understanding regarding a certain matter, you have to seek God about it. You have to be willing to put in prayer time and study time to have a clear understanding of scriptures and the spiritual essence of other things. God has also given you spiritual leaders to help you on your journey in life. Never ever assume anything, even when it comes to

A VIRTUOUS WOMAN'S PRAYER IS JESUS FILL MY CUP

people. You should always get a better, godly understanding. "...In all your getting, get understanding." Stay Encouraged! Stay Motivated! Stay Close to God! Have a blessed week!

YOUR PERSONAL NOTE TO GOD

_____
_____
_____
_____
_____
_____
_____
_____
_____
_____
_____
_____
_____
_____
_____
_____
_____
_____
_____
_____
_____
_____
_____
_____

WEEK FORTY-SEVEN

VISION

Focus: This week I encourage you to meditate on vision.

Scripture: "...Write the vision and make it plain on tablets..." (Habakkuk 2:2)

Declaration: I believe that my vision will manifest real soon.

Prayer: God, I am so thankful that You gave me the vision, and I have written it as You instructed me to do so. I pray that You bless it to manifest real soon. Amen.

Message: You must have faith and confidence in knowing that if God gave you the vision and instructed you to write it down; He is not that kind of God that will not bless it to come to past. There is an appointed time for that vision of owning your own business, writing a book, becoming a school teacher, a doctor, a lawyer, a model, an actress, etc. to manifest. Just hold that image in your mind. The Bible says, "Though it (the vision) tarries, wait for it..." While you are waiting, don't be so quick to share your vision with others. There are some people who surround you who are not happy for you, and they really don't want to see you live out your dreams. I encourage you to play it safe by simply not sharing. Stay Encouraged! Stay Motivated! Stay Close to God! Have a blessed week!

YOUR PERSONAL NOTE TO GOD

_____

_____

_____

_____

_____

_____

_____

_____

_____

_____

_____

_____

_____

_____

_____

_____

_____

_____

_____

_____

_____

_____

_____

_____

_____

WEEK FORTY-EIGHT

VICTORY

Focus: This week I encourage you to meditate on victory.

Scripture: "But thanks be to God who gives us the victory through Lord Jesus Christ." (1 Corinthians 15:57)

Declaration: I believe that I have the victory.

Prayer: God, I am so very thankful for Your giving me the victory, and I thank You for being my Lord and Savior. Amen.

Message: I want to let you know that no matter how it looks or how hard it may be right now, it's still going to work out for your good, according to Romans 8:28. You may have been losing in the first, the second, the third and fourth quarter of your life, but God is going to cause you to win in the "fifth" quarter. God knew your beginning, your middle, and your expected end before you were ever created. The things that you have been facing are all a part of His plan for your life. You'll be able to testify about the things that you have encountered, and your story will help other people. The reason the devil hasn't been able to take you out like he wanted to with the attacks that he has launched is because of Jesus Christ who lives on the inside of you. "Victory is yours." Stay Encouraged! Stay Motivated! Stay Close to God! Have a blessed week!

YOUR PERSONAL NOTE TO GOD

WEEK FORTY-NINE

WISDOM

Focus: This week I encourage you to meditate on wisdom.

Scripture: "For the Lord gives wisdom..." (Proverbs 2:6)

Declaration: I will use the wisdom that God has given me every day.

Prayer: God, I pray that You bless me to operate in wisdom all the days of my life. Amen.

Message: I want you to know that wisdom is a gift, a benefit that you should value and thank God for. It is a privilege and an honor to possess such gift from God. If He has given you wisdom, He wants you to operate in it. If you lack wisdom, I encourage you to ask God for it. He will bless you with it. We are living in such a cruel world, and having wisdom is much needed. You will need to use wisdom to make some of the best decisions in life. Yes, wisdom is needed for that very crucial decision that you are about to make in your life this week. Stay Encouraged! Stay Motivated! Stay Close to God! Have a blessed week!

YOUR PERSONAL NOTE TO GOD

_____

_____

_____

_____

_____

_____

_____

_____

_____

_____

_____

_____

_____

_____

_____

_____

_____

_____

_____

_____

_____

_____

_____

_____

_____

WEEK FIFTY

WORSHIP

Focus: This week I encourage you to meditate on worship.

Scripture: "...worship the Lord in the beauty of holiness." (1 Chronicles 16:29)

Declaration: I will always worship the Lord, our God.

Prayer: God, You are worthy of my worship. I pray that You are pleased with my worship. Amen.

Message: God loves when you worship Him. The Bibles says that we must all worship Him in spirit and in truth (John 4:24). This is because God is spirit, and you have to be free in your spirit in order to offer Him sincere worship. It is so important to get your mind off everything that is going on around you and focus totally on Him. You have to release unforgiveness, anger, strife, and all other things that will hinder you from getting His attention through worship. You may have a desperate need right now, and you need God to move suddenly in your life. I encourage you to make time to go to your secret place and worship Him throughout this week. Stay Encouraged! Stay Motivated! Stay Close to God! Have a blessed week!

YOUR PERSONAL NOTE TO GOD

WEEK FIFTY-ONE

WORTH

Focus: This week I encourage you to meditate on worth.

Scripture: "...Her worth is far above rubies..." (Proverbs 31:10)

Declaration: I will value who I am and know my worth.

Prayer: God, I pray that You allow me to see myself the way you see me. I know You value me as your daughter, and I ask that You not let people mistreat me and devalue me. Amen!

Message: You don't have to entertain anyone who makes you feel like you are not worthy of anything because of your past experiences or shortcomings. I encourage you to keep striving to become your best self, asking God to help you to grow each day. You should look in the mirror, give yourself a hug, and start embracing who you are. God has certified and qualified you to fill the position as a virtuous woman. Starting now, value and appreciate who you are, and don't allow others to devalue your worth. You are an important, smart, special person to God. Stay Encouraged! Stay Motivated! Stay Close to God! Have a blessed week!

YOUR PERSONAL NOTE TO GOD

WEEK FIFTY-TWO

ZEAL

Focus: This week I encourage you to meditate and focus on zeal.

Scripture: "For I bear witness that they have a zeal for God..." (Romans 10:2)

Declaration: I will have a zeal for God and the things of Him.

Prayer: God, I pray that you bless me to keep being on fire for you and having zeal to do your will and not my own, according to your righteousness. Amen!

Message: No matter what you will ever face in life, you must always remember to put God first, and He will make sure everything else falls in place. God wants to see your heart's desire to please Him and not man, woman, or child. Don't be sidetracked by those who have no desire to please God. Don't be overly concerned with the things of the world. I encourage you to "fall in love with Jesus" and make Him smile by simply submitting to His will. If you don't already have zeal for God, get serious about getting it so you can move forward on your journey in life with joy in your heart and praise on your lips. Stay Encouraged! Stay Motivated! Stay Close to God! Have a blessed week!

YOUR PERSONAL NOTE TO GOD

_____

_____

_____

_____

_____

_____

_____

_____

_____

_____

_____

_____

_____

_____

_____

_____

_____

_____

_____

_____

_____

_____

_____

_____

_____

When you are at the brink of giving up, just know that God will give you that much needed strength to press on.

"Stay Encouraged! Stay Motivated! Stay Close to God!"

To learn about Yolanda Marshall-Nickerson's other books and how to book her as a speaker for your next event, you may visit her on the web at www.yolandamarshall.com.